El Greco

16 BEAUTIFUL FULL COLOR PRINTS

(PLATE ONE)
ON THE COVER: *Laocoön* 55⅞" x 76"
1604–1614 (Cossio); c. 1606–1610 (Mayer)
National Gallery of Art, Washington (Kress Collection)

Art Treasures of the World
100 SIXTH AVENUE · NEW YORK 13, N. Y.

El Greco CLEANSING OF THE TEMPLE

National Gallery, London

(DOMENICOS THEOTOCOPOULOS)

EL GRECO

(1541–1614)

Greco, 1541?–1614

TEXT BY JOHN F. MATTHEWS
Lecturer, City College, New York

THREE GENERATIONS AGO, the artist presented in this portfolio had been neglected for centuries. There was a time when histories of art, if they mentioned El Greco at all, merely set him down as a mad Spanish painter who deserved to be ignored.

Within the last hundred years, however, the revolution in art and taste which led to what we now call modern painting, also led to the rediscovery of El Greco. Today, this sixteenth-century artist stands at the very apex of world popularity.

But the curious history of Greco's reputation is no more paradoxical than the elements which went into the mak-

ing of his life. To begin with, this most "Spanish" of painters was not even a Spaniard.

Domenicos Theotocopoulos (nicknamed "the Greek") was born about 1541 in the island of Crete. Formerly an outpost of the ancient Byzantine Empire, Crete had suffered many humiliating invasions; and by El Greco's time, it was the property of Venice. Culturally, however, the island still looked east, toward lost Byzantium (where art and Christianity took the form still seen in Greek and Russian Orthodox churches). Sixteenth-century Cretan painting, for instance, had little in common with the secular and "realistic" art of Renaissance Italy. Instead, it was

1

the Byzantine art of the icon, or holy image—whose object was not to represent life but rather to create religious emotion through severely stylized drawing and design.

This was the tradition in which Theotocopoulos grew up and became a painter. Then, at twenty-five, he turned his back upon it.

About 1566, El Greco went to Venice—a city which had adored and perfected an art of the flesh. He went to work in the studio of Titian, who epitomized a lush neo-paganism we might expect the young icon painter to find objectionable. It was a splendid place to learn the techniques of Renaissance painting, certainly, but how could El Greco work there?

(One possible answer, of course, is that by then Titian had begun to give up concentrating on noblemen and nudes, and was turning to the same religious subject matter with which we identify El Greco. By 1566, the impact of Protestantism had roused the Catholic world to a new enthusiasm for sanctity and martyrdom. And so, to match the changing social atmosphere, Renaissance art tacked to sail with the rising wind of the Counter Reformation.)

At any rate, Theotocopoulos transformed himself into an Italian artist with incredible rapidity. He absorbed Titian's techniques of painting and portraiture; experimented with the daring light-and-shadow contrasts of Bassano; and acquired Tintoretto's skill at dramatic composition. (From the latter, too, he learned a unique method of painting from wax or clay models, whose construction apparently took the place of preliminary sketches.) Within four years he advanced upon Rome, hailed as a new Venetian master—and seven years later, he left Italy entirely.

Toledo, where El Greco settled in 1577, was one of the prime centers of Spanish Catholicism. Seldom, perhaps, have the energies of a whole city been devoted so fanatically to otherworldly objects. Not only was it a headquarters for the Inquisition, but its population was made up largely of priests and monastics. The resultant atmosphere, though dangerous for heretics, was superbly suited to El Greco's genius as a painter.

Soon after his arrival, he was commissioned to do a picture for the priests of the Toledo Cathedral Chapter. When he finished it, the Fathers asked him to make some changes, which he refused; whereupon they tried to avoid paying him, which made him famous. Suing for his fee, El Greco won an arbitration which decided, along with the price, that his *Espolio* (plate four) was "one of the best pictures ever seen."

From then on, his story had little in common with the familiar romantic nonsense about "starving artists." His work was in constant demand, and handsomely paid for. And the result, naturally, was paradox.

In a city devoted to asceticism, El Greco lived for nearly forty years, it is said, "so as to enjoy all pleasures at once." This man whose paintings deal principally with the miraculous ecstasies of martyrdom and self-imposed suffering, occupied a sprawling twenty-four room apartment, where he even maintained a private orchestra to accompany his meals. And though he was a specialist in pictured piety, it is interesting to note that he may never have bothered to marry the mother of his son.

For a final paradox, it should be remembered that El Greco was in many ways what we should nowadays call

El Greco ST. FRANCIS RECEIVING THE STIGMATA WITH BROTHER RUFINO *Hospital de Mujeres, Cadiz, Spain*

a "commercial artist"—painting to please patrons who very often gave him strict instructions as to what each picture was to contain. (See plate 6.) A commercial artist with this difference, of course: that to every subject he stubbornly brought the special complexity of his own artistic heritage and genius.

Along with his personal vision, what makes El Greco's work unique *technically* was his ability to fuse the two seemingly antithetical modes of Italy and Byzantium. In Crete, he had learned the pictorial discipline of the icon maker—which taught him how to organize a picture as a highly stylized design, aimed at creating the psychological effect of *revelation*. (See plate 16.) In Venice, on the other hand, he had mastered an art which dealt with the representation of *events* and *characters*—a dramatic, realistic art, which attempted, not so much to make you *feel* like a saint, as to *show* you the saint in action against a background of the human world.

Many artists before him had used one or the other of these approaches in art. El Greco, uniquely, did both. His special achievement was to capture the essence of a Spanish generation which held life on earth contemptible in comparison with the promise of eternity—and which yearned to achieve a mystical union with God through self-denial and martyrdom. To accomplish this, El Greco intensified the story-telling canvas of the Renaissance with astonishingly forceful stylized elements from the icons of his Cretan homeland.

The result is neither madness, nor, as some have thought, a miracle. It is simply great painting.

2

Commentary

Note: The chronology of El Greco's work is uncertain; where there is no general agreement, our sources for the dating of paintings in these commentaries are usually the works of the two outstanding Greco scholars, Manuel B. Cossio and August L. Mayer.

COVER (PLATE ONE)

LAOCOÖN

1604–1614 (Cossio); c. 1606–1610 (Mayer)

National Gallery of Art, Washington (Kress Collection)

55⅞" x 76"

CONSIDERING EL GRECO'S MASTERY of late Renaissance techniques of painting, it is interesting how little sympathy he seems to have had for the subject matter of much of that art. This *Laocoön*, for example, is the only pagan theme in his entire catalogue.

And even here, among the legendary figures of classical Greece, he does not choose to paint a typical Renaissance interpretation. Instead of the customary amorous wood-nymph, or naked Venus, he picks an incident which is strangely analogous to the theme of the Catholic Counter Reformation: the extermination of those who are disloyal to the gods.

Remember that Laocoön was a Trojan priest of Apollo. Not only had he offended the goddess Athene by warning Troy against the famous wooden horse, but he had also outraged his own god, Apollo, by lecherous impropriety in the precincts of the temple. Like many priests of the Renaissance, the family of Laocoön was felt to have profaned its holy trust; and the ensuing punishment was both swift and terrible. It has been suggested that the theme can be read as a pagan parallel to Christ's cleansing of the temple.

Following the custom of the time, Greco gives the story a local setting: it is not Troy in the background, but a city which resembles Toledo. And now that the libertine yet truth-telling Laocoön writhes in agony, the deadly Trojan horse advances without opposition to inflict its punishment.

Compositionally, the whole picture seems to whirl outward from the head of Laocoön—a dispersed, centrifugal canvas. What helps hold it together, of course, are the figures of Apollo and Artemis buttressing one side, with the upright, struggling body of the son (and the downward hook of the sky) limiting the spectacle on the other side. And the whole picture, too, is unified in terms of color, through the pervading browns and greyish-greens.

PLATE TWO

HOLY TRINITY (1577–1578)

Prado, Madrid. 118⅛" x 70½"

THEOTOCOPOULOS arrived in Rome about six years after the death of Michelangelo. There is a curious legend which claims the young Greek was driven from the city some years later because, after studying Michelangelo's famous frescoes in the Sistine Chapel, he arrogantly volunteered to replace them with something really worth looking at!

Whatever El Greco's opinion of Michelangelo (at seventy, he referred to the Italian as a "good fellow, who didn't know how to paint"), his own first work in Spain shows marked traces of the earlier master's influence. Here, for instance, in a Holy Trinity (Father, Son, and Holy Ghost as a Dove), which he painted for the little church of Santo Domingo el Antiguo, the effects of his Italian studies are clearly seen in the picture's conception and composition.

Notice, for instance, how everything centers on the powerful figure of the crucified Christ. Quite as much as "the exuberant robustness of the anatomies," this trick of focusing the picture on one dominant element reminds us of Michelangelo and the Renaissance —and it is a practice which El Greco eventually tended to abandon. In late works, he not only treated various portions of the picture almost as separate compartments (after the Byzantine fashion), but he also dispersed the attention-getting elements outward toward the edges of the composition, rather than inward toward a single center. (See plate 16 and cover.)

Even in his first year in Spain, El Greco was obviously a superb artist in his own right—but not yet entirely in what was to become his own way.

PLATE THREE

CLEANSING OF THE TEMPLE (detail)

1584–1594 (Cossio); after 1604 (Mayer)

National Gallery, London

THIS COLOR PLATE is a segment of the monochrome picture in the text (page 1)—a brilliantly planned expression of the confusion and panic of the money-changers, who try unsuccessfully to escape the whip of Christ's punishment.

The upward straining figures make a frantically explosive series of movements away from the menacing Christ. But simultaneously, a series of strongly marked horizontals contain and counteract this movement—a series which begins with the bent arm of the standing man at right; is repeated in the edge of his yellow garment and in the arm of the fallen woman in the center; and again in the back of

3

the tautly stooped figure in the corner, who is trying to lift his heavy money-chest. As Professor Leo Bronstein puts it, in his monograph on El Greco, "all this action and counteraction, advance and recession, very exactly conveys to us the impossibility of escape!"

PLATE FOUR
EL ESPOLIO (1579?)
Cathedral, Toledo. 112¼″ x 68⅛″

THIS IS THE PICTURE that made El Greco famous in Spain. It was painted a year or two after his arrival—on order from the priests of the Toledo Cathedral Chapter, who commissioned a "despoliation of Christ by the Roman soldiers."

El Greco organized his picture in the Renaissance manner, focusing attention on the massive central figure of Christ, or more particularly, on Christ's brilliant garment, at which the fingers of his captors are already clutching. (This is the famous "coat without seam" for which the soldiers cast lots rather than destroy it by division; and it was important to Catholic symbolism, as representing the unity of the Church.)

Around this vividly clothed Christ there circles a scheme of independent yet associated figures and heads, each of which leads the eye on around to the next, and then centripetally, back to the blazing cloak in the center. And notice, too, the complex economy of El Greco's design. All that we see of the cross, for instance, is the fragment at the bottom of the picture; but its line is exactly paralleled by the outthrust arm of the jailer who holds the rope. And this arm, in turn, forms a suggestion of the completed cross, as it passes over the arm of Christ, which is extended in benediction over the audaciously foreshortened carpenter below.

When El Greco's clients saw the finished work, they decided that it was not exactly what they had bargained for. They began by asking the artist to repaint certain details which they considered "unorthodox." To their surprise, probably, El Greco stubbornly insisted on the validity of his own personal vision, and flatly refused to make the desired changes. Whereupon the priests accused him of violating his contract by passing off an inferior piece of work, and tried to withhold payment.

El Greco, instead of giving in, promptly took the matter to court. The result was not calculated to encourage those sentimentalists who like to believe that great artists are always misunderstood in their own lifetimes. The case was arbitrated by a Toledo goldsmith named de Montoya, who consulted other experts, and then not only awarded El Greco the sum of 3500 *reals* in payment, but went out of his way to remark, in his decision, that the painting was actually worth more than that—was literally priceless—and deserved the title of masterpiece.

It was a judgment with which subsequent critics have not been tempted to disagree.

PLATE FIVE
ST. JEROME AS A CARDINAL
1571–1576 (Cossio); last period (Mayer)
National Gallery, London. 23″ x 18½″

HERE IS A PICTURE which illustrates the paradox of El Greco's style.

On the one hand, it is a vivid and strikingly personal portrait. The great scholar who translated the Bible into Latin, and whose terrible pen was such a scourge to his enemies, is seen here not as usually portrayed amid the severities and self-imposed penalties of his fervent monasticism, but rather in the uneasy majesty of his scholastic eminence. The earnest and sincerely troubled face of the learned Saint is a triumph of that penetrating realism of which the Renaissance was so proud.

But on the other hand, the devices of Byzantium are here, too— the symbolic distortion and elongation; the almost compartmental separation of elements (the face, at its enormous distance from the hands and books); and the stylized geometry of the composition as a whole.

The result of this unity of diverse means is a work of awe-

inspiring dignity; a portrait in which the subject is conveyed, not merely in terms of an understanding of his character, but also in terms of a suggestion of his significance.

PLATE SIX
BURIAL OF COUNT ORGAZ (1586)
Church of Santo Tomé, Toledo. 191⅞″ x 141¾″

EL GRECO LIVED IN A SPAIN which considered life a sin, and only death adorable. Mystic and church militant combined, in his generation, to prove and preach salvation through suffering and obedience. "Inhibit your feeling for earth, so as to achieve heaven."

In 1578, Theotocopoulos was commissioned by the parish priest of Santo Tomé to paint the story of a miracle which had occurred in his church, and which aptly illustrated the proper relationship between life, death, and heaven.

It appears (from an inscription at the bottom of the picture) that a certain fourteenth-century Lord of Orgaz had led a life of such piety as to win himself an incredible glory at the moment of his expiration. In the presence of assembled nobles and ecclesiastics, he was honored by "the descent from open heaven of Sts. Stephen and Augustine," who personally undertook the burial of his body.

This was what the artist was asked to put onto canvas—and the result was something which El Greco himself called "my sublime work."

Notice the deadly silence of the witness. Every face tells its private story of pious assurance. For the moment, heaven has opened to earth, but nobody is surprised, or stunned, or even particularly curious. It is an overwhelming event, perhaps, but received by men who have known all along that death is more glorious than life. Even the little flickering hands are merely indicating the obvious.

Meanwhile, in heaven, everything is active, passionate, dynamic. Assisted by an angel, the embryonic soul of Orgaz mounts through a whirling vortex, pushing up past the thoughtful Virgin and the company of pleading saints. Everything absent on earth finds expression in heaven.

One wonders if this is El Greco's *statement* of faith, or a commentary upon it. If earth be so inglorious, why does St. Stephen look so sullen and resentful, and why does St. Augustine, alone of the figures below, look so tenderly sad at this duty of burial?

The more one looks, the more one wonders.

PLATE SEVEN
VIRGIN WITH SANTA INES AND
SANTA TECLA (1597–1599)
National Gallery of Art, Washington (Widener Collection). 76⅛″ x 40½″

MAN IS NOT SATISFIED to be earthbound. The term itself implies a kind of failure of the spirit; as though gravity were not merely a descriptive law but a downright penalty.

Consider, for instance, how the language abounds in images which associate the better part of life with defiance of the tugging earth. Our spirits soar; we hope to be free as birds; we are uplifted, and have our moments of elevation.

For the mystics, this soaring of the spirit is all that truly counts in the universe; even the body joins in yearning upward. For the orthodox, heaven is not merely a state of mind, but a state of corporeal existence, aspired to through the resurrection and elevation of the body itself. (Among mystics of the East, for example, this state is even held achievable here on earth—whence come those legends of levitation and suspension with which travelers from India used to regale the wondering Occident.)

This theme runs through El Greco's work with a conviction and assurance that is seldom more magnificently demonstrated than in this picture. See, for instance, how easily and how naturally this lovely Virgin asserts her holiness through the simple elevation of her body in space. Indeed, so skillful and persuasive is the picture that there is not even anything of assertion here; there is merely the elegant statement of fact. The Virgin literally floats upon air.

PLATE EIGHT
ST. MARTIN AND THE BEGGAR
1597–1599 (Mayer)
National Gallery of Art, Washington (Widener Collection). 75⅛″ x 38⅜″

THE DISTORTION OF FORMS is as old as the history of art. In ancient Byzantium, for instance, artists often indicated the importance and holiness of a subject by an excessive lengthening and verticalizing of the figure.

In El Greco's hands, this expressive device took the form of an uprushing elongation that twists and contorts the body out of all proportion. Here, in the picture of the knightly St. Martin dividing his cloak with a naked beggar, notice how lightly the latter's huge figure rises from the earth—as though the dainty, almost feminine feet did not so much *support* the upward thrust as *depend* upon it.

It is by such qualities of the bodily forms, more than by the gestures and facial expressions of pity and benevolence, that El Greco conveys the spirituality of the episode. The modern viewer is tempted to fall into the error of a literal reading of this art (and, indeed, of much of Christian art). But Greco's conception of the underlying Christian virtues of compassion, brotherliness, and charity is more evident in the nobility of the figures, and especially of the marvelous white horse, than in the features, which remain detached from the particular action.

PLATE NINE
HOLY FAMILY (VIRGIN OF THE GOOD MILK) 1594–1604 (Cassio); 1590–1598 (Mayer)
Hospital of San Juan Bautista, Toledo. 44⅛″ x 41⅜″

EL GRECO LOVED TO PAINT MYSTERIES—to seize upon those cryptic moments when the human spirit stands revealed in some equivocal relationship with divinity. And it is a mistake to think that, for him, these were always moments of agony or ecstasy.

Sometimes, as here, the mystery is as sweet and serene as the blue of the sky—as tender and thoughtful as the face of a father. For this is a picture of parents, full of the wonder and gentleness of loving adults in the presence of an infant.

And the marvel of it is not only in the faces. It is seen even in the fingers of those long, delicately protecting hands, which encircle the child so lightly and with such reverence. One senses here the holiness, not only of this family, but of love itself.

PLATE TEN
ST. LOUIS, KING OF FRANCE (1586–1594?)
Louvre, Paris. 46″ x 37⅜″

HERE AGAIN, one has a sense of confronting the unexpected. Considering that we usually think of El Greco as an artist who painted sanctity at the very peak of its intensity, who would have expected him to present a monarch-saint in so melancholy and intimate a fashion?

Indeed, as Leo Bronstein has pointed out, it is a curious conception of this mighty warrior of the Lord: as a thoughtful, rather awkward man, whose crown does not quite fit, and who carries the symbols of his majesty with a kind of hesitant uncertainty, as though unsure how they should be handled. And how odd, that the page-boy who helps the king dress, should appear more self-possessed than his master!

Paradoxically, too, there is nothing very saintly about this king. His face is a *good* face, the intensely genuine face of a man who wishes to do the right thing, obviously—but there is nothing here (or anywhere else in the picture, for that matter) which conveys the impression of holiness. The quiet, rather sad dignity of the portrait is derived much more from the king's humanness than from any overwhelming impression of his spirituality.

Finally, the pictorial treatment is as frank and direct as the choice of pose is cryptic. Whatever the meaning of the enigma, the figures are drawn deliberately and precisely; and El Greco's smooth brushwork renders the textures and surfaces very realistically, with painstaking attention to detail.

PLATE ELEVEN
CHRIST ON THE CROSS
1590–1600 (Cossio); c. 1580 (Mayer)
Louvre, Paris. 98½″ x 70⅞″

CERTAIN SUBJECTS were especially popular with El Greco's patrons, and probably with the painter himself. He was a kind of specialist in pictures of St. Francis, for example, and turned out at least sixty-seven paintings of this particular saint. In a sense, he practically cornered the market for St. Francises, just as Matisse, in our day, has pretty well monopolized the trade in odalisques.

What it comes down to, of course, is that in the days before printed reproductions were available, artists like El Greco often did version after version of their most successful paintings—sometimes with the help of assistants. The *Espolio*, for instance (plate 4) was so widely admired that El Greco did some fourteen similar paintings with the same title, along with eleven St. Jeromes and nearly a score of Annunciations.

They were not mere copies of one another, however. They were always variations; large, inexhaustible themes like the Crucifixion, for example, lent themselves to endless re-exploration and re-statement.

The version shown here is interesting in that it continues the old medieval custom of including the artist's patrons in a picture of a holy subject. Here the donors—two gentlemen in contemporary Spanish dress (who probably presented the painting to the church for which it was made) are seen worshiping the figure of Christ crucified. Their unctuous piety is portrayed just as they probably hoped it would look to the world; and the bland and elegant body of Christ is exactly the proper object of their very correct adoration.

But behind all this there looms the anger and menace of a threatening sky; alive with a swirling turbulence which makes a vehement commentary on what Bronstein calls "the showy self-righteousness" of the scene in the foreground.

Indeed, one cannot resist quoting this critic's magnificent summary remark about these figures: "They are floating fragments of superficial exaltation, on the ocean of a portentous and truly exalting sky."

PLATE TWELVE
ST. JOHN THE EVANGELIST
1594–1604 (Cossio); 1600–1604 (Mayer)
Prado, Madrid. 35¼″ x 30⅜″

"THE FACE IS SOMEHOW FRIGHTENING; one has seen it before, and knows the consequences of that twisted and complacent visage. Nothing can touch it; reason cannot urge it to compassion; it merely responds to argument with the softest suggestion of fanatic superiority, while it testifies to its own adolescent unassailability by reference to its own fabulous evidences."

So wrote a modern dramatist, who insisted upon interpreting the faces of El Greco's saints as though they were to be understood as contemporary character studies.

Scholars, however, remind us that El Greco probably intended no such reading of his work. For his contemporaries, the meaning of such a picture was not likely to be discovered in its impact as a piece of ironic portraiture, but rather in terms of its theological significance—as a demonstration of certain conventional themes. In this instance a saint illustrates the utility of faith by means of a miracle, which incidentally, confirms the fact that he is truly a saint.

More specifically, the reference is to an apocryphal event in the life of St. John the Evangelist, whom the Emperor Domitian tried to murder, during the Saint's visit to Rome, by putting poison in the Sacramental Cup. The poison, however, revealed itself by turning into a serpent, which benevolently saved the Evangelist and his companions by killing their enemies.

5

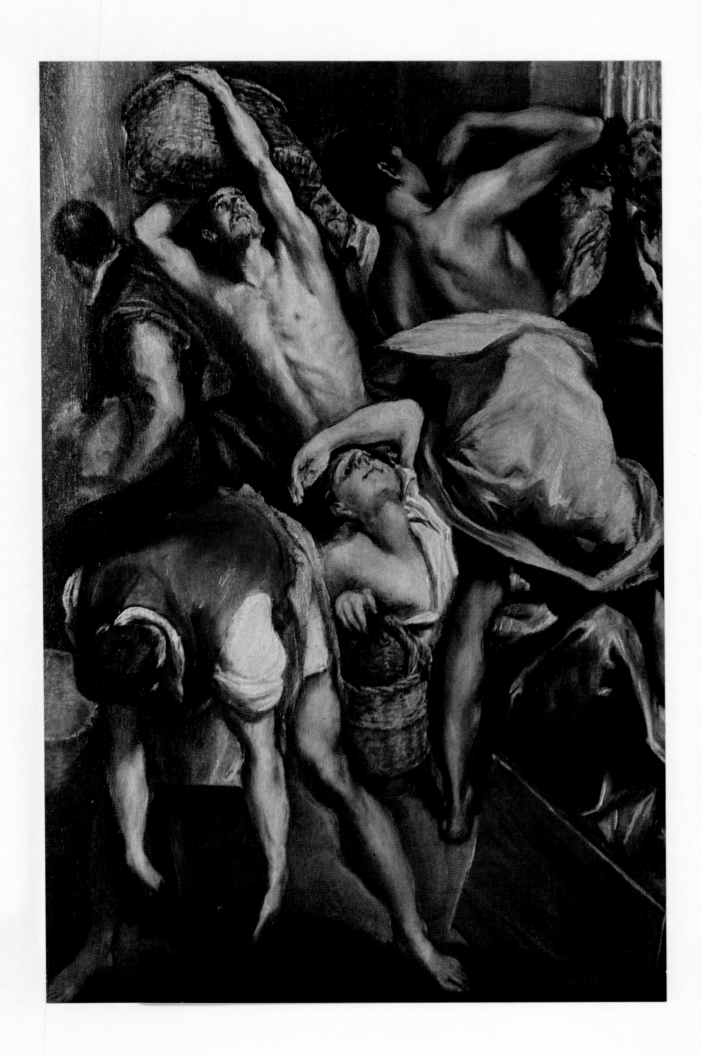

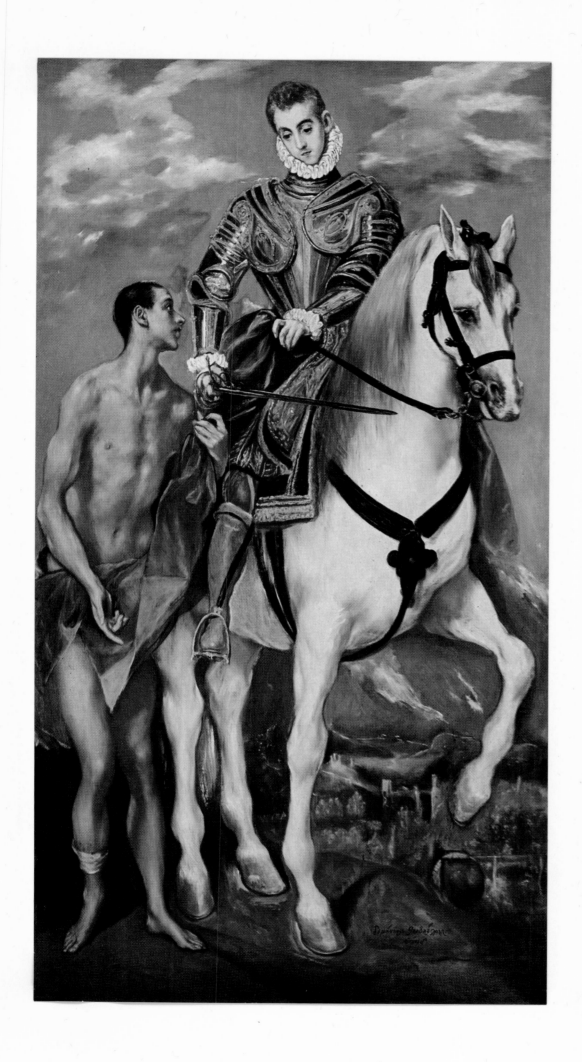